CW00758705

Pocahontas in Ludgate

Mike Bannister

ARROWHEAD
PRESS

First published 2007 by
Arrowhead Press
70 Clifton Road, Darlington
Co. Durham, DL1 5DX
Tel: (01325) 260741

Typeset in 11pt Laurentian by
Arrowhead Press

Email: editor@arrowheadpress.co.uk
Website: http://www.arrowheadpress.co.uk

© *Mike Bannister 2007*

ISBN: 978-1-904852-15-5

All rights reserved. No part of this book may be reproduced, stored in a
retrieval system, or transmitted in any form, or by any means, electronic,
mechanical, photocopying, recording or otherwise, without prior written permission
from the author or Arrowhead Press.

Requests to publish works from this book should be sent to
Arrowhead Press.

Mike Bannister has asserted his right under
Section 77 of the Copyright, Designs and Patents Act 1988
to be identified as the author of this work.

Arrowhead Press acknowledges the financial assistance of
Arts Council England, North East.

Arrowhead Press is a member of
Independent Northern Publishers.

Printed by Athenaeum Press, Gateshead, Tyne and Wear.

TO

SUSAN, TIMOTHY, HELEN, WILLIAM

and all their loved ones.

One wing-beat of the heart can hold
centuries, heights of a third heaven,
a stumble in a dream, a waking
lost in a small familiar field
within sight of the lights of home.

Sally Purcell

Acknowledgements

Some of the poems in this book have appeared in *Other Poetry* and *Envoi* magazines.

Cavaliri di San Marco won 3rd prize in the *Crabbe Memorial Poetry Competition 2005*
Yarn Hill (early version) won *The Elizabeth Cochrane Memorial Prize* in the *Thetford & Wymondham Open Poetry Competition*
Singing Stone won 2nd prize in the *Crabbe Memorial Poetry Competition 2006*
Ironbridge Coalbrookdale was joint winner in the *Shropshire Libraries Ironbridge Bicentennial Poetry Competition 1979*

Sue Bull, my daughter, read these poems, made the connections and created the fascinating pictures that transform our book into a small thing of magic. I am also indebted to Robert Petty, John Withers, and Alasdair Aston, all of whom offered much valuable comment, and to James Knox-Whittet for his insights. John Watts, The Suffolk Poetry Society Portfolio Group, Cafe Poets of Halesworth, Bungay Poets, and *Other Poetry* Magazine have provided encouragement over the years, and together with Joanna Boulter and Roger Collett at Arrowhead Press, have helped to make this book reality. Above and beyond all these, I want to thank Ann, who has given me peace, and the time to read, to dream and to go on writing.

The cover picture is by courtesy of the artist Mary Ellen Howe and the *Virginia Historical Society*, Richmond, Virginia, USA.

'One wing-beat of the heart...' is taken from
Sally Purcell: Collected Poems ed. Peter Jay. Published by *Anvil Press Poetry* in 2002

Contents

Wellsprings

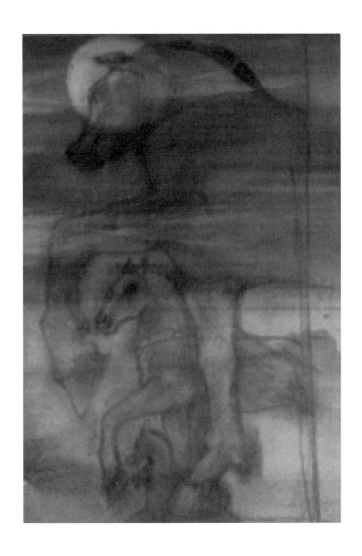

Town Clock Metfield

Five centuries, the deep heart's
unwavering pulse furnishes the nave;
filed cogs and freighted cables,
made for a time of giants, conjure
the hours, the waking bells.

This is a movement born of stasis;
the pendulum and nodding pawl lend
governance to each spindle's momentary turn;
the sweeping hands raise fresh minutes
from the soundless well of time.

The day's round scope and charter
is reckoned here, our entrances and goings out
measured, as if perhaps the common will decrees;
good time is something we should try to keep,
against the world's unwinding.

Venice – A Masque in Autumn

She is a dream portrayed in water-light,
bride and lover, desirous, magnificent with age;
her towers and palaces seeming to melt away
in the seductive, many-coloured sea.

Harlequinade: motley of craft, curved moons
in burnished cherry wood, and rakish dories,
fleet rowers from an Arabian frieze, leaning
forward, dripping with mist and thrown spray.

Ashore, the pressing crowd, a jostle of traders,
souls contingent on the sea, somehow charged
with the imminence of landfall, or a putting out,
Argonauts, alert, counting on the flood.

Sure, all the gods of light and fire are here
content to forget at last, and to forgive, while
Peace, beyond the treasure of a thousand kings
flits in and out, disguised as Columbine.

The Deer Pool ~ *for Ann*

This small treasure in the hills of Tarn
shimmers like the half-closed eye of earth itself,
brim-full, watery and wild green;
                    one cool thing in a burnt land.

At first light, they ghost up here,
out of the harbouring trees, and half-kneel
by turns, to slake themselves,
                    calf, hind and stag.

Come sunrise, they seek a cool breeze
on the high ground, leaving certain signs;
the sweetest hint of musk
                    hangs on the air,

where narrow feet have pricked
the wetted clay, the trampled green recovers,
earth-coloured in the morning heat.
                    Time of the Canicule:

nothing seems to move, save
deep below; some strange nymphaean pulse,
renews the source, softly,
                    with the purest welling.

Cavaliri Di San Marco

Were these the four that drew bright Phoebus
through the constellations, their clanking harness,
savage music, echoing through silence ?
                            Quadriga – all the horse that ever was.

Avatars, far larger than life, in bronze
the supreme rendition of elemental forces
clenched in the act of starting forward.
                            Was ever power, between motion and stasis
                                    so achieved, all standing ?

The livid gape marks scarcely-harnessed fear;
something short of panic primes the sensual, almost lewd
physique of slung sinew, veined withers, rolling thews.
We half expect real thunder from such hooves,
or lightning from the stone.
                            Was ever so much live beauty snared,
                                    its raw power made manifest ?

Like bellowed furnaces, the nostrils flare
summoning the foundry pit, all scorch and glare;
the furnaceman's own juice, pitched in,
a sweat-stink, mimetic of equus, of animus,
patina's nitric seed, green, gold and silver,
down the years; age upon age of slow ensaltment.
                            Never was craft or cunning turned
                                    to realise so much majesty in tribute.

And all this time, lords, kings and conquerors,
wanting certitude, took them for spoils of war and peace
as if possession might alone confer, however brief its span,
some kind of parallel magnificence.

Postcard From A Distant Town

By air, another trim perspective,
a market square, high tower and carillon,
a moat with waterfowl, in perfect tones;
a picture, yes, but not the feel, exactly;
nothing of the people, shades and faces,
the distant music, smoke and dust.

Between the lines, read absence
and a summoning; the wishful thought
of you between us, talking late, fathoming
under stars, a more particular sense
of place, our table quite disorderly
with olives, good bread and Friulano.

At Kingairloch ~ *for Bill Summers*

Beside the forest fence you work
the soft black loam, conjure order
out of chaos; long summer hours
dissolve, in the tender husbandry
of nature's great green clock.

Your neat rows proclaim
creation, divine and inexplicable;
the seasons' ceremonies unfold;
root leaf and seed, harmonious
with rain and light, *become*.

For what's a gardener but a poet
in some other guise? His pacings
rhythms, rhymes and subtle sowing?
Are not one's end-stops like
another's harvest crops?

Is not the careful reckoning
of time the guarantee of almost
perfect fruits in each of these
two heavenly pursuits?

Greenstreet Again

On Goathland Fell

At freedom's end,
in ripe September,
we quit the clamourous fishing town:
the chill breath of a grey sea;
tide and the people
ebbing.

On Goathland fell,
the wide heath shimmers, murex-tinted.
Caped in heather; curled
in the bank of the old lane and each other,
we drift among soft purple waves,
drowsing.

Sleep comes warm and easy in our arms,
with dreams of strange territories;
landfalls and discoveries yet unmade;
prospects, projects to raise,
and roots to put down;
settlements.

The play of insects in the scented air
leads me, wakening, to your smile,
and to the pleasant understanding
that nothing of this could be,
without your loving;

Surely, it came to me,
love's foundation is with us now;
together, in communion, here,
on Goathland Fell.

The Hedge Flail

Here, in a blizzard of slivered shoots, rides
Giles, high on his Diesel-driven tower of strength
the great McConnel Double-headed F-19.

Caution! Before God, it fills the lane,
this roaring thing, cuts deep, disjointing
branch from bole; strikes down the unformed
fruit, compelling autumn to unnatural ends.

The gin-trap, gleave and flensing iron
are not more terrible to me, than this sad treason.

Caution indeed! The sweet air turns sour,
old boundaries recede, forced back so that our
line of sight allows insane velocities.

Yet, seeing further, we may see less well,
how these pale flitterings might yet conceal
some unexpected thorn.

Night Ride

Along the road from Hinderclay
by Stowlangtoft and Liver Mere
the ivy python writhes on dying trees,
feeds upon wormwood, gains ground,
out-shapes the hawthorn and the oak;
a weird guising. Strange things flicker
where the headlight strobes
in and out the racing dark.

Last night I saw the hippogryph,
a one-legged lizard-bird, a giant hare
about to span the county in a leap;
a lean outlandish knight with lance
and shield was there, and gone again
to shadow, haunting the waste,
the silent woods, from Hinderclay
by Stowlangtoft and Liver Mere.

Green Willow ~ A Worcestershire Idyll

Winter in our seventh garden,
a ladder climb, a stretch, a cut
or two through tangled salix
opens the heart of it, shapes it down
to the bud shields, outward facers;
in some strange way the sway of it
inclines the mind to memories...

Beyond the fence gate, early morning,
I pick up the steady zzzip of his saw
above the seethe of the lower sluice,
see a willow-pole lean, then swoop down,
half in, half out of the pool, and him,
lugging it for a while until it drops free
from the pollard, still up his ladder, poised,
oblivious, working out the next move.

Dragged ashore, he strips it of leaf
and twig, gauges, cuts and starts up
again; works all morning, moves along,
each crown harvested with axe and saw
until he calculates he's cut enough.

Sunrise, next day, he starts there,
all noise of him lost in water fall;
clears nettle under the sour apple,
spade-slices into black earth, lifts out
a heap of gold roots; puts in a footing
of river stone, and as the light dies
he stands quiet, then rakes it over,
true as he can judge the thing.

Come Sunday, four by six, he sets
the poles, tamps each with brickends,
hard down, levelling the long split
carlines, steady and four-square.
The 'run' he firms with smaller stones
then parges concrete to a subtle fall
with gullies and a hidden soak-away.

Goes fishing then; comes in late
to talk over supper, embraces sleep
noisily, sighing like an old sea-lion
adrift on the tide of his atonement.

Next 'day off' he sheathes the frame
in rippled iron with diamond plates
to spread the force of pounded nails;
makes 'furniture' from red clay pipes
to channel meal and swill along,
then plies with bristle brush and tar,
a gleaming finish to his handiwork.

The first rain falls, a new pig snoozes,
pink-trottered in a cloud of yellow straw,
and where the roof-drips come to ground
small rainbows tremble and dissolve.

Again

After all this time, we expected changes,
but not the scale diminished; as if the land
had slipped inwards, closing down the stream,
hampering the swirl between pebble-shoals
and the shelving, alder-rooted deeps.

The *Wellingtonias* seem nearer, almost grand,
casting a green half-light on the stone bridge
where we two lean, not speaking much;
lost in the sweet remorse of coming home.

Tom Burman's field the cricket green
is unkempt, thistle-bound. His Jersey byre
planked in the saxon form, is now a 'unit';
windows busted, floor gone, as if a slow war
had ravaged through, leaving no prisoners.
These woods are mournful, bearing still
the tawny shade of winter. Not like it was.

Yet something moves, coming through,
cracking twigs; two lads, twelve and ten
maybe, the taller with a fag in his palm,
forcing the tangle down to the river's edge;
their imaginary Africa? Could have been us.

They both look up and wave, climb round
for 'Dr Livingstone' hand-shakes.
We try, and fail, to talk about the old ways.
Their eyes shifting at our 'sixty years ago'
then the small one says: *"There's still
this massive black carp in the mill-race;
never been landed!"*

In our day it was a giant eel, half-buried,
watching from the sand, jawful of green
wire gimps, our own Grendel. Strange,
and somehow wonderful, how it continues,
this mystery of the source, its tutelary ghost,
finding another form, another time.

Ars Moriendi

Death came to me sidelong
from among my friends;
an old familiar, so far
denied and yet persuasive:
promises me safe transit.
And, willing to the end,
I surrender my self.

I dream the world beyond
is as it was before, save for
the ash upon my sleeve.

And being no more, unseen
among the living, I feel content
to re-acquaint myself with
the risen dead.

The Souterrain

Reflections on Three Subterranean Light Installations by James Turrell
Yorkshire Sculpture Park 2005

After Turrell graduated in 1966, he rented the former Mendota Hotel in Ocean Park, California. Initially sealing the building from the sound and light outside, Turrell set about experimenting with projected light within the darkened building. Gradually he made small openings in the paint or blinds covering the windows – THE MENDOTA STOPPAGES – to introduce shafts of moon and sunlight into the space. This important period of experimentation and development, which included research with a perceptual psychologist as part of the Art and Technology Programme at the Los Angeles Museum of Art, provided the basis necessary for all subsequent works.

(i) Gray Day

My guide surrenders me to a darkness
whose limits are at first unclear. I wait,
uneasily, for the dawn of new perceptions;
cones and cortex seeding a narrative.

A wall of rich purple waylays the eye;
on either side, twin pools of snow-light,
quiet, unwavering, as Plato pictured it;
a cave wall, wanting shadows.

In time, no longer bound captive
by the dark. I draw forward; the lilac panel
opens, translates to cool zero, a purple void,
worrying, vertiginous.

I grasp the rim of it and gape, then realise
at last, the promised view beyond will not
reveal itself, this day or any other.

Out of this diminution, I speculate,
find fresh interiors, admitting slowness
as one aspect of what it is to learn.

(ii) Ganzfield

I move through a milky flood,
a theatre of pale indigo and sapphirine,
having no fragrance, sound or calorific force;
it swirls down through the optic pools,
invades the far capillaries.

If this inundation has a source,
it lies elsewhere, outside the far
wall, smooth to perfection, iridescent.

Rays of pure colour fire each surface;
all interfused, the seer somehow *becomes*
the shade; were he to cut himself,
would even bleed the same.

No room for darkness here.
In this low cell, some lost flower god
has rendered the sky's cerulean with
sweet-blush purple, to make mysteries,
perfect as the Bell Flower, Periwinkle
and Forget-me-not.

(iii) Wedgework

To be so close, down here, to Steel Town,
is to recall colossal radiance, vast billets
of not-quite-molten metal, being slow-hauled
from furnace to forge.

Here stands one such, in sharp lines,
turned half-towards me. A painted cenotaph,
pulsing orange light. Measured to deceive,
it transmutes into a room within a room,
a blue-gold memory of past glories.

Once, giants were here, artisans
working the dark with grace and fortitude,
dealing in fire, dying young. Their hundreds
haunt the foundry stones.

Underground, I reconsider
the power and degradation of the past
and wonder, by what unearthly chain of trial
and fortune, and in what strange foretelling,
these things should come to light.

Deer Shelter Project
(Yorkshire Sculpture Park, January 2006)

That low mound sports a neat new
parapet, a dry stone footprint, Turrell's
secret palimpsest, in parkland under trees.

Underground, in simple white,
a room translated from the Minoan, lined
round with seats of stone, its plain walls arching
to a void, a lidless eye, chiselled square, open
perpetually to the light of fading stars.

Stretch out: up there the oculus
shines milky blue, draws out the mind
through solar haze, so many planetary miles.
You begin to gauge, to sense the far Empyrean,
and even as you think it, one solitary mote
of thistledown, each filament alight with
universal fire, comes drifting in.

Afternoon: daylight floods across
the north and eastern walls, a gilded square
attenuates, folds, clockwise, passes over you
and moves on, as by degrees, you accept this
moment of being; the sole diurnal
rider, inside a stone kaleidoscope.

Dragon Song

Before Ossian sang, or Finn came striding
from Galway to Kintyre, before Brendan sailed
his boat of hide, brought him Christ a-voyaging,
I was young. I ruled the tide in Ailort by Arisaig,
hawked fire, burnished my scales on grey shingle,
harried salmon and deer, slept away time
among birch woods.
                  Now in far Logres lie my bones,
small wonder for children, or for bards to sing;
the dream, of a dream, of a dream.

A Field of Folk

Late Fisher

A shadow in grey and green
and silence glides the levee,
comes to rest where the reeds'
whisper gives him dominion;
a dark mirror in a bowl of leaves,
with crayfish, bent on chalky
expeditions, combing the soft swaithes
of maiden hair, deep down where
shouldering Rainbows swim.

He folds himself, threads line,
tugs filament, spittles the knot,
chooses his fly-form; the night,
still warm on his face, drifts in
with fall of light. Waiting now,
he watches the rise and tumble
of late gnats, notes how they
are sipped through watery rings
into a thousand small oblivions.

Quick wrist and forearm
barely turn, the cane whispers,
flies back, sighs, stops, arcs
forward, hissing – thirty foot
of flight, feather, wisp and barb
floats out along the ripple.

Silence, time and light fuse
into a single warp, a presence;
nothing moves but the fingers
of his slow left hand, drawing in,
a foursome reel, looping and
letting fall the wet silk strand.
At last he is composed, and ready
for the start of sudden game.

Dropping The Pilot ~ *for Russell Bower*

Your sturdy cutter heads for home,
shrinks to a hyphen, a full stop, loses
itself among silos, wharves and cranes
where you attend to other work;
somehow, we feel diminished.

The river dilutes itself, becomes
the sea; out of hazard, the pulse
picks up, desire and memory driving us
to find that undiscovered shore.

We measure, chart the lines,
watch the cyphers flicker in the dark
make metaphors of things unseen;
not certain of ourselves, but sure,
in heart of hearts, when we return,
you'll steer out to meet our craft
and claim your share.

A Midnight Call ~ *for Amber*

No more than half-alive, I thread the dark,
   pick up the jarring telephone; warning myself
      no good news ever came from calls as late.

And through one hundred miles of silence
      a breathless voice of seven years begins
         ' *Is it you?* '
   and reassured, continues
         ' *I've seen it, seen it for myself;*
         remember the saucepan,
         and the wishing star beyond?
         They are all up there, now
         look out your window, quick! '

I do, and there as ever, over the print-works roof,
      Polaris and the Plough, somehow renewed,
         wink through a haze of indigo.

What can I do, but praise her will to seek
      and find, before we share a good night wish?

Wide awake, I drift between the Pleiades,
      the Hunter and the Swan;
unwilling, just yet, to leave behind
      the cosmic wonder cloud
         she brought into the small hours.

Fen Woman

Prospect: a distant tower
somewhere far off,
a barn, a line of trees
like decorative pins
brailing down the light.

Within this cloudscape
you set your seventh tent
where the earth is fruitful;
long levels of swart loam
deep sedge, a shift of sand.

Nothing much intrudes
between your self and heaven;
you made the bright border
the ring of flower light,
about the family coat.

No intervening ridge or vale
disputes the whisper
of the restless sea; only
the sense of your prevailing
turns it all to song.

Little Buddha Of The Snows

In the silence of a white garden

he sits, smooth head leaning forward.

Behind him, the trees whisper like water,

far away. He recollects the voices of children,

music of nations; and prepares himself

to fathom the exact and particular

sound of snow falling.

My Friend Sapphire

As the ferry draws close, a small white hand
waves from the cabin glass; already she is alert
to the pungent ripeness of the lagoon, its chimes,
and memories of other landings, other shores
where weeds like mermaid's hair, in languid coils,
drift on the sleepless waves of morning.

Along the watery maze she flickers,
window to window glass, like water-light
on soft white stone. The sunbeams flare
on grand piazzas, fountains, statuary,
and people stand, numberless as the doves,
to stare in wonder at the City of the Sea.

Late on, filled with all the brilliance
of her hours, she climbs to her attic room,
with small shutters under flower-painted beams,
and turns her thoughtful gaze, far out across
a silent, terracotta sea, to catch the golden angel
on the campanile, walking the sapphire sky.

The Blind Man Of Tomen-Y-Mur

Under the Roman camp at Islyn,
where leaning walls hold out against
rough hill and waste, he works, collarless
in a once-white shirt, the rest all black;
face and arms peat-coloured, as if
a looking-glass would be for him
a thing of no great consequence.

He follows an ordered line
of mounds, scattering rough spoil.
Like a rower in his stride, rhythmic,
he shifts the sweet fertility, disposing
the float and fall of each new levelling;
his silver fork-tines feeling out the line.

Our clatter seems to stall him,
midswing; he cocks an ear, sidelong,
as if to gauge the way of our approach;
our waving makes no difference.
He stands awhile, then sings out
a word or two in the Old Tongue,
before continuing.

Something alternate confers
dominion here. Some quiet confederacy,
of wind-song, or slant of rain; perhaps
the inclination of the land positions him
until the light's glance fades, warms him less;
draws him at last to the hearth-side.
through his own perpetual night.

Autodidacts – Notes For A Manifesto

(i)
Who learns not, lives not,
and living not, continues dying...

(ii)
To lay open,
to identify, and know affinities;
to let the senses discern
the sufficiencies of narrative,
is to feel the springfire,
the pulse of being.

(iii)
Words pressed on the white leaf,
the promise of a bound cypher
the charm of libraries,
fire to the hunter's charge,
the essence of life's quick spark.

(iv)
Having no knowledge of set lists,
nor having skipped, for some master class,
the course prescriptions.
we follow, for all time,
the live mind's sequence of epiphanies,
like travellers enjoying liberty
in some undiscovered land.

.

Pocahontas in Ludgate

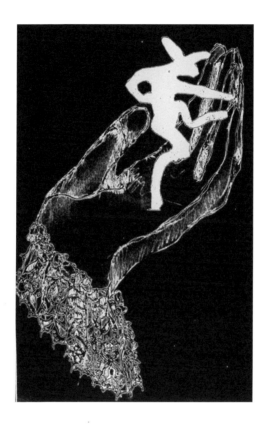

A sequence of Seven moments in the life of Mato-aka
Daughter of Chief Powhatan King of the Chesapeake Algonquian Tribes:
how, as a girl, she was observed by the settlers;
her intervention in the 'execution' of Captain John Smith;
the political significance of her marriage to John Rolfe;
her meeting with Ben Jonson, at the Bell Yard, Ludgate, in London;
her attendance, as guest of King James, at the Twelfth Night Masque of 1617;
her final meeting with Captain Smith at Syon House, Brentwood;
and her untimely death at Gravesend some days later.

I – Antemasque Jamestown

"Why look you so, and all turn dumb?
My presence rather should invite,
And aid, and urge, and call to your delight."

There by the turbid river,
three ships, sprung in the mud and heat:
a scrape of earth, and pole houses,
that would become a city,
named for some faraway king.

Mato-aka, child of the forest,
unafraid of the interlopers, the listless
pallid ones, their skin-smell foreshadowing;
strangers, who earth their seed-corn
when the moon is down, who threaten
among the villages, who beg for food
and cannot fend;
                          she outstares them all

with a smile, lets slip
the featherwork of her veil, and
                          in puris naturabilus,
palms to the warm earth,
makes a slow hand-stand, sinewing upright
in perfect balance, controlling
the moment,

then, pointing, she arches,
silent, lithe and artless,
into cartwheels, through the open roughness
of that unmade town.

43

II – The Deliverance Of Captain Smith

There was a camp
beside the mudflats of Potomac
with the Long House of Powhatan,
strong against blizzards.

In there, the war band,
the women, the children, all silent;
and the chief, staring, and the wife of the chief,
who brings a bowl and turkey feathers
for the prisoner to make clean his hands.

Despised, feared, hated, powerless,
bound in hide strips; the knots cut him.
He is cold, hungry and afraid,
only the children return his smile.

Then the stone is rolled out;
the killing stone. The filthy, hair-faced
trickster is thrown down.
An unforgiving hardness
cramps flesh against skull bone
and measures the end of feeling.
He smells, but does not breathe
resin, smoke, sweat, and fear.

Suddenly, a roaring gale of voices,
a nightmare of primal shrieking
deafens out the world; his sweat-sore eyes
catch the stone axe, rising, the axe
of slaughter; and again:
a haunted silence.

Then a scamper of bare feet,
a childish shout; his head, throat, neck
and bound frame are covered, shielded,
claimed, by the arms and warm body
of the girl Pocahontas.

III – A Peace Between The Nations

"Already, with her sight, how she doth cheer,
And make another face of things appear."

Not in the ceremony of the copper ring,
by which the clerks aspired,
to save her wild soul for eternity:
but later, maybe, at Varina;
she and old Rolfe,
firing the tanglewood,
grubbing out the charred roots,
working the black earth,
in the joint and public sacrament of tending seed.

Through this, imperial scavenge
waits upon the plough, fear gives ground
to expectation, and rapine halts its rout,
while time, and wise husbandry,
become their compass star.

Brave innocents, whose league,
fearless and unconditional,
holds back the trade of cruelty, destruction,
turmoil, depravity and swift death.

This was their golden harvest,
cropped from the dry seed of fear;
a divine transmutation,
by which these two secured
a Peace between the Nations.

IV – Pocahontas In Ludgate ~ The Bell Inn 1616

"I have known a princess and a great one,
Come forth from the womb of a Tavern...."

He stoops out of rain and into darkness,
the reek of old sack, new leaf,
damp air, and candle smoke;
where seacoal crackles in the grate.
His old campaigning cloak
drips and drips. The sherry gleams
and swift anticipation bids him start.

'Master Rolfe, Sir, your goodwife,
this... Princess of Virginia'
who, in an upper room, is called
from the forest of her dreams
and enters, robe drawn tight,
into a gale of voices, stew of smells,
the dim cell, where sits 'Poet',
who is also 'Friend of James'.

Huge, unsightly, great of jowl,
with hands that have known rough work;
the eyes yet gentle, burn as if his heart would say,
'All that you feel and fear, Princess, in this
strange kingdom of deceits, is in me contained.'

Dark eyed and with royal complexion,
bronze, honey, amber, pearl and gold and jet,
her open gaze endures this great ugliness,
meeting each brisk interrogation
with equal parts of modesty and grace;
being content with silence, and serene,
while he, speechless, for near an hour
attends her
'as if some waking dream,
or spectacle of strangeness was,
there and then, engendering'.

46

V – *Masque Royale* ~ *Twelfth Night AD 1617*

" Wonder must speak or break: What is this?
Grows the wealth of Nature here, or Art? "

Music:
in a far forest of stone and steel,
at the Long House of the English king;
fanfare and silence resounding
through the hall with twenty doors,
by flamelight, shimmering
in crimson, green, in blue and gold,
hundreds wait upon the long silence
before the first strange blaze of spectacle.
Hush..... secrets, secrets.....Hush.

Now see The Sun King, and his Lady Moon,
amid their preening warrior-lords
like forest cocks a-strutting; and see at his arm,
that strange Virginian Lady with her twelve Indians;
and she is pale and beautiful and near to death
while courtiers, behind their double faces hid,
consider her and are amazed.

And here again is the poet story-teller,
the "Great Tun" who leads them all, through flattery
and adulation, past riot and beyond, toward cool reason
and a sense of common wit,
before he calls them down to dance.

From revels, then, to revelation
they sound their way. The wheeling crowd,
with rhyming feet makes patterns, measured out
in verse, Coranto, Galliard, and Ring;
so to dissolve, this happy while,
all the false categories of caste,
allowing the common ALL to touch,
to lay hold, *'on mysteries more removed'*.

47

VI – Syon House ~ A Reconciliation

"I will call you father,
As you, bringing fear to our people,
Engaged mine."

To visit her in those last days,
at the house beyond the city,
came he, to whom she had given life,
and a loving close to worship.

Out of time and the other world of death,
where fire had taken him,
this unkempt, ancient, raddled apparition,
pathetic, grandiose in his cups,
confounded her.

And was it pride, or sorrow,
more than wonder, stirred in her,
after a silence of hours, the need to ordain
a more exact relationship,
one of love, tempered?

And in the darkness,
before she lost herself in sleep,
did her tears, for this wild, good, silly man
signify, at last, some realisation;
that there would be no more meeting,
upon the short road ?

VII – Pocahontas At Gravesend

"All must die; 'tis enough that the child liveth."

After the festivities, the twelve nights
her ship, the home-going ship,
waits for a wind on the grey river,
and all that bitter while,
in a cold and airless lazaret
the daemon fever strips away her life,
sure as heart of hind falls
to the hunter's blade.

Then the ship, *The George*,
puts back to lay anchor at Gravesend;
its melancholy freight is lowered to the gig;
a lifeless form in a canvas shroud,
against which spray from the oar blades
rattles like musket fire.

Without horn or drum, she is
sung to chancel and the yawning clay.
In the candle-light, her child wails
while sorrow bathes his father's jaw.

And the last dream of Mato-aka,
Princess of the Spear Fishers,
is of her journey to a warm woodland;
where children dance about the Summer Queen
in the shade of apple trees.

She moves towards the rising of the sun,
to the dominion of the Great Hare, King
of the Four Winds, keeper of the skin bag
from which all people will
sometime, rise again.

Findings

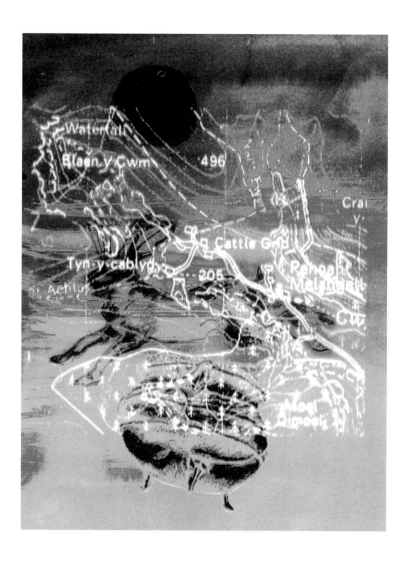

The Singing Stone ~ *for Helen*

Shore walking, heron-hunched, so long now;
the youngest reckoned, at first, it was about

filling my coat with grasps of sea grit, weed
and pebble; until they found a sailor's pearl,

a fairy shield, could tell a cowrie from a unicorn
and flint charms, which the sea, for good luck

had softened and sucked its way clean through.
This late winter brings a singing stone

from under the storm down Dunwich way;
a squat grail, half-tunnelled, whose secret eye

sings to my second breath, a frail note
of elfin song, higher than wash of waves;

like instant silver, drawn from its dull ore
gleaming sea-bright in the falling shade.

On Candle Dyke

(i)

A place of uncertain balances,
a flood contained, levels barely held,
quiet seepages, the sweetness of decay,
slow flux of ends and of beginnings.

If there is flow here, it is imperceptible.
October evening, windless, the mute reeds
purple in sunset's after-bleed.

A mist spills over Thurne levee,
silvers the drained marsh, cloaking
the rise and fall of secret hierarchies.

(ii)

Downstream: the flicker of an eelman's lamp,
and silence, fractured by his capstan pawl.

The long chain lifts, parting the waters.
He rides across, handing his low boat,
up-ends each diamond-netted snood,
fathoms the silver lode.

Shuffled by lamplight, his writhing
hoard, pin-eyed, serpentine, conjures,
even in captivity, long-forgotten fears,
way beyond our grasping.

(iii)

Midnight: no noise of any kind,
then, through the lantern's beam
like wandering spirits from another world
a silent frieze of more than twenty swans
glides out of darkness into dark again.

The drove leads down below the bank,
lower than water, reeds and fish; Atlantis
under stars, until a more insistent glow,
the intimation of a town on fire, gathers itself,
into the roundel of a harvest moon.

Yard Sale

Beyond the Cenotaph at Lidice,
the rain eases; a farmstead, desolate
with rank weed, pale clay and shallow pools,
is pitched about with little theatres of the lost
staged, for the day, on flapping polythene,
on tail gates and faded gun shrouds.

Here's poverty, a clutter of not-quite
perfect things, the universal tack of
flea-markets, trunk and garage sales;
chipped crystal, prints and imitations,
scuffed books, bench-tools, worn clothes,
clocks that have slept a hundred years,
the paraphernalia of discontinued lives.

But most, I feel the muted redolence
of violins, rose-lacquer under grime and dust,
some quarter-size for tiny hands,
some with frayed bow-hair, bridges cracked,
others with no strings at all.

I listen for the slow tunes, airs of longing
that would charm a winter into golden spring.
Where now the wedding songs, the village
feasts and pastorals, the fire lit dances,
the gypsy songs of passion and despair ?

Silence, but for the slow soft pluck
of raindrops as all that handsome pine
endures the last effronteries of time,
and the first chill winds of Autumn
come worrying the uplands of Bohemia.

The Sea Is Coming Back

"Now corn grows, where Troy once stood."
Ovid, Heroides

They say the sea is coming back,
north ice melting, glaciers waning,
flooding the land from Lynn to Little Port
and there I saw a thousand hollow ships,
with fires flaring, and a wall of reeds.

Word's out. The sea cuts nearer now,
covers the fen; salt foam, white on grass
lighting the green land, rich in horses.
The long dyke, the fired barrow grave;
all there is to find of ancient war.

I've heard the winter tides roar closer,
filling the wide bay where some lithe
warrior, brooding by his tent, watches
the sun rise over sea and land, rides
his battle ride through a hail of bronze.

These times, the channel's broader
that harboured in a fleet of ships for
her whose name is written in the land
by Homer's Town, beyond the Fleam, time
before time, so many thousand years.

They say the sea is coming back
where Gog-Magog was lost and won
and the proud voyagers, their sail-flax
battened to the breathing of the sea,
went south, and took the tale to Troy.

The Cauldron ~ *A Discovery*

This, with two out of three legs,
a thousand times utile, broken, disowned,
outcast from another time, they found
by Tanat late one summer.

A sense of something
mildly mythic attends the finding,
deep in the silence of Powys;
a broken grail in the hedgerow,
half of all its roundness gone.

What of the finders, then ?
He, questing, unclothed, feral almost
sleeping among leaves; and she,
the woman in strange raiment, who sang
in perfect metre, of flowers on a silver branch,
finder of the missing fragment.

Now after twenty years, mended,
the wholeness of it, gathered, made
magical; an ancient wonder-work:
vessel of rebirth, and redemption,
bestowing love; the one true
hallow of their bond.

How To Cook A Whale Found Dead
(a found poem)

Ingredients and Utensils:
a beached whale, not dead too long
knives, cedar ropes and seawater
round stones for the cooking boxes,
store boxes, firewood, and long strips
of cedar-bark for *tied-in-the-middles,*
stir-sticks, ladles, awls.

Helpers and Dignitaries:
Hunters first, to cut and haul, wives to chop and cook,
the daughter of the hunter who found the whale,
father of the one who found the whale,
your Village Chief, his family, others of rank.

In front of the invited ones, bestow,
upon the daughter of the one who found the whale,
the ceremonial name *Place-of-the-Blubber-Cutting.*

The canoe procession follows the one
to the spot where he found the whale.

First, the Father of the Hunter praises the whale;
how wonderful, how full of delicious blubber,
making it a grand *something*, taking his time...

The Hunter's Daughter makes the first cut,
tenders to the chief the choicest part
of dorsal fin, signifying rightness, justice.

Now all the hunters go to work, strip out
fathom-wide sheets, working from the neck along,
leaving the tail intact; each guest is given several
according to rank, and what is left,
the women gather up.

To make an end to the ceremony, everyone
in turn comes forward to take a small piece
of raw whale tail; they stand in silence,
chewing, quietly remembering the whale,
and the driving power of the whale.

Balanced on canoes, all the pieces
tied securely, you make the difficult
journey home. There you split the meat
and blubber into strips, four fingers,
then one finger wide, ready for cooking.

Make the round stones red hot in a big fire
on the *down-home-beach*. Fill the cooking boxes
with clean sea water, and lift in the stones, one by one;
as it boils, put in strips of whale-meat,
changing stones, cool for hot, over
and over, about twelve hours.

Ladle off the rising oil, *proof-against-rain*.
Store it cool. There is no end to its uses.

Offer cooked meat to all the guests;
give them more, it goes well with
wild-berry rolls and while the eating
singing and dancing continues, cook again
whatever remains, stirring, stirring.

Last of all, thread the blubber pieces
on cedar strips; hang them to dry in smoke
beneath the rafters; when the rain-days come,
boil these to make the hot dish called
Eating-boiled-blubber-tied-in-the-middle.

Penmaen Pool ~ *December 1980*

Remember the first night
of the last winter of the old decade,
after the long summer harvest
had come to an end in storms?

And two swanbirds
looming upstream in the darkness,
white on the slack tide like
foam flecks, breaking loose,
growing out of the tide race
over from Borthwnog?

Into the gale they butted,
pausing sometimes, to filter
a final slippery something
from the swirling silt, quartz grit,
punished alder leaves, and slivers
of unseen gold, that flicker
seawards from Gwynfynydd.

Stepping sideways, first she,
somehow I knew it must be 'she'
waiting for him to have his last dabble,
then both together, climbing the mud bank
for the marsh, to sleep there, fronting
the ice-wind that hammers down from
high Brithdir, until the eastern hills
roll slowly into morning.

Once

Inside The Hollow Hill

Two hundred fathoms out of sight,
beneath the turf of Pitman's Mound
a dark blue web of silence winds;
strange warren, where hard lives
were traded for the wages of the world.

This hidden shaft, chill fall,
pierces the inner earth;
a core of fire-damp and foul air
choking each fissure.

Down there, an inky slime
embalms the skewed form of
one who never found the village lights:
Tag-disc 'one one nine'; his obelisk, a tangled pile
of leaning timber, rough wheels
and rusting wire.

Blackness: the eyes cannot engage;
panic revives my waking dream,
howls for some fixed co-ordinate, craves
sense and sanity out of nothingness.
Not now. The sun is set forever
inside the hollow hill.

In the dark, an icicle,
like some blind timepiece lets fall
its metering drops; wears down
the ancient print of fossil ferns.
An echo dies.

Here is a stone jar, left empty
by some thirsty half-dead man-crab
beside a spike of iron dust
where the rats came last,
to finish up the tallow.

And far in,
along that low-beamed gallery
the full-boned frame of a buckled
pit-horse stands, immured in backfill
marking the end, the timely stopping point;
seam, beast, lode, and human labour
finally worked out.

Yarn Hill

Over Iken by the silent fen,
between orchards and the low land;
a mound, a landmark, a meadow,
raised crested with fine trees;
an eminence, hand made, formal,
insistent on the eye, as memory
fold back time's winding sheet.

Here it was always known,
and told to tell, down four score
native dynasties, ever in keeping
for the young to hear, a spring
of memory that never dried,
as ink upon the printed page.

Upon Yarn Hill, they say,
after the great rising, the fire,
the slaughter and severing of heads;
after a red layer of ash and bone
and shattered samian had settled
on all that was left of three cities;
after the legions made victory, and revenge,
her people, in desolation, entombed
Boudicca, Queen of Cenamagni.

Only the melancholy curlew keens
about this hill of mourning, and in the heart's
imagining, her song is of a sea wind
sighing in the reeds.

Somewhere, inside this hollow hill
she sleeps, in cell of stone; fine gold,
white bone, a coil of chestnut hair,
all wrapped forever in forgetfulness.

Landfall

South of Tahiti, three months
beyond the reef, on salt fish and breadfruit,
we work our toy contraption, every stick and string;
inking the blind chart through storm and windshift
adrift beneath the unmeasured sky; each night
precipitate, with its cross of stars.

Ten days and nights we chased 'Cape Flyaway'
until the south wind dispersed him, leaving us desolate
on the pale waves; the leadsman poised,
with nothing to call.

Round Michaelmas, we find signs:
kelp weed, driftwood, with barnacles,
a seal even, asleep on the endless tide,
and by the forenoon bell, October sixth,
we hear the lookout singing *Land a' lee!*

That same day, sunset, we crowd the deck
and see it clear: a forest, smoke rising,
high hills, a river, a new Eden, waiting.
All night we stand off, cautious, without sleep.

Come dawn, short sail, we steal close in;
counting canoes, people, houses, fires.
The sail makers sew covers for the swivel guns.
In ten fathoms, sand, silt, He calls *Let go;*
chain roars, the cable snubs: deliverance.

First over is the pinnace, then the Master's yawl,
and down we spring, bent low to loom and blade,
giving way, in time together, pulling steady
until the lookout whispers *Indians,* pointing west.
The Master steers inshore, intent on a meeting;
the pinnace waits, all covered, in reserve.

Up through the trees we find the houses empty,
then from the far side, five dart shrieking down
as if to claim the boat; panic, alarm, more shouts;
we run, wade, push off in a sweat of terror, breathless,
gliding with the stream, while more come on,
naked, in a roar, hurling spears.

The order comes to load, and fire high,
but they, not knowing what to fear, press forward
and I am the one, who in a rage of hate takes
more deliberate aim, causing the first to drop,
and all the rest to stand and stare.

Ironbridge Coalbrookdale

Once was a valley, flayed,
rifled, all its wealth stripped out;
the earth turned sour
with spoil and cinder.

Hell's furnaces respired,
hawked up a yellow cloud
mucus-thick, red-stained,
salting the eyes like sweat.

Time moved to the pulse and tumble
of trip beam and bellows, the grind
and clatter of harnessed water.

Cupolas bled, hot as the sun's gut,
their incandescence cooling
to black brittle for the dawn shift
to prise away, strange forms
out of black sand.

Across the narrows,
peculiar shades are cast;
artisans, diminutive against
the beams, with wheel and lever,
hoist and wedge, piece up
this weird contraption of false elm,
first to connect, and then divide
the inching buttresses.

Once was a generation, bribed
with false coin from the green fields,
bowed long in the hearth's maw,
getting mutations on damp clay,
dying young; a woeful flux,
the final reduction, man to beast.

Stranger, if you pause to watch
Sabrina, glancing through,
reflect upon the stream of years;
this Iron Cenotaph proclaims
The People of the Great Reserve,
who, in their hundreds, foundered here.

Auguries ~ 2001

On the balcony of Europe,
time of Orion wheeling,
four flares, away to the east of greenish light,
some desert storm, perhaps
renders me wakeful.

Search memory; back to the start of it,
the stream of events already set in train;
another assassin, hero, fanatic, downs an Arch-Duke
for the umpteenth time, rolls us all way beyond
the traditional line in the sand?
After the comedy, what next?

'Viewers may find the following images disturbing.'

If only we would – sufficiently.
We remain, cordially inattentive,
oblivious of the bite; of what is meant
but never said, by the button masters;
slaves to premature retaliation,
front of house types, not quite clued-up,
yet eager, with quaint first broadsides,
to speak, in sepulchral tones,
ill of the not-yet-dead.

The air is thick with counterfeits;
*'Sanctions are imposed. Aid will not move;
arms, yes, but not food. Ambassadors, not hostages,
are exchanged. Forces deployed.
Capabilities, eroded with no collateral'*.
The truth died first, forget it.

On every side we are degraded,
incapable of saying how, out of hubris
or innate stupidity, we fail to entertain
the slightest dread of these familiar signs,
here in the dark, on the balcony of Europe;
time of a crescent moon, time of another war.

East Anglian Interlude ~ *(October 2002)*

Twelve days, sea and air seem
barely to move. Moon and Sun
steer close in, threatening flood tides.
In a season of utter stillness, I wake
to the sound of a distant bell.

Chill sunrise, in perfect quiet,
long shadows and low rays
engrave the pale dew-light.

After harvesting, dull gold
roulades of straw stand sentinel
among trees and ghosts of trees.

The whole wide sky is pale,
without cloud or chalk-line
fighter-traces: geared for war
young guns are under orders,
flying south and further east.

For once, we wish them home;
wish their fighter howl would re-echo,
to break our silence and confound
the auguries, forestalling, for
good and all, an evil harvesting
across the weary sands of Uruk.

Djinn *(Baghdad 19.3.03 – 02.30Hrs.)*

A hill of dust wells out, swirls
to make the gaping maw of Kronos,
city wide and heaven tall, then doubles
ten times with electric speed; becomes
a crouched colossus, arms raised
about his cloud-head curls of fire,
Efrit, the most fearful, is unloosed.

Out from under the shattered palaces,
the blown cellars of the *Radwaniyah,*
out of ignorance and greed and fear
boils the grim uncoiling of our fate.

He is the cindered spawn of rapid fire,
colour of earth and blood, a wild wraith
of matterless death, a gas cloud, pounded
with the stench of metal, mortar, mortal
flesh and bone, a laughing after-echo.
frenzied, hysterical, revelling in war.

If all the seers of all the nations came
to draw him down into a flagon made of
brass, what hope for humankind
of his confining? What hope, we might
unweave the shame of his unleashing?

Praise Poems

How To Make A Gondola ~ *for Hollie Yasmin*

Leave the house early
before the others are about,
find the steps beside the bridge
that lifts us over the *Gesuiti*.

Sit in the sun awhile
and watch the lights dart,
soundless through and under
the cool stone arch.

Wait there
for the roaring fleet,
its boatmen calling and singing
as they slide into the wide Lagoon:
Sandalo, S'ciopon, Mascareta e Gondola, ...

not to watch them, directly,
so much as to sense their passing,
and admire the scimitar curve of high prows,
the cutwater's folding, the soundless slide
of the wash and the widening wave, the slap
of the lap on the green stone at your toes:
not watching, I say, so much as
taking account of it all.

Now trot ahead, enjoy the sun;
passing the book-binder's window,
the toymaker's workshop,
the soft snow of acacias in palace yards.
Be astonished again, surprised at the sight
of the *Miracoli*, divine in fretted marble,
and so, by turns and bridges,
to the *Campo Giovanni e Paolo*.

In the square, have your picture taken,
drink lemon soda,
then chase around with the doves for a long time;
follow them as far as you can, laughing all the time,
not quite flying,

until you happen on, and, breathless,
pause to collect,
three fallen quills and a branched
frond of tamarisk.

Lean on the bench,
under the grand facade of the *Ospedale*,
explore these four found things;
dream, and weave them with small fingers,
not even seeming to think
about what they achieve or amount to,
until it comes to mind;

no longer any one of boat, bird, feather,
sun, or tamarisk; suddenly, a distillation
of lift and grace and balance,
the quintessence of a whispering
wave kissing, dark cherry wood
crescent moon and mirror,
light as air, afloat before your eyes,
a perfect '*Gondola*'

which you entrust, at once,
to your ancient friend,
who recognises it
exactly for what it is,
and promises to harbour it, safe forever.

The Pearl Of Orinsay

Out of the night she comes,
veiled among racing clouds,
a simple round of gentle light,
soft, and flawless among stars;
turning the wide sea silver.

Who sleeps and wakes again
far, far away, must feel content;
the self-same moon that lights
his longing dream, lets fall this night,
a touch of pearl on Orinsay.

The Puppet Theatre ~ *Norwich St. James*

We are among mysteries, made
from old paint, rough string and whittlings;
soft smiling manikins, with eyes that long
for love, ministering in company.

Imagine the fantastic; a choir
of childhood friends and strangers:
Kind Noah and the Norman King,
Pale Unicorn, Dido, all in tears,
the Leaping Hare, with Punchinello
and the Rose Princess, inclined
in postures not quite real, wanting
no more than whispered words
to stir them suddenly awake.

Scantlings: names out of time,
roof-beams of the ancient town:
Losinga in his stone boat, Dame Alizon
and Chapman bold, the Grand Jurnetts
and Shady Meg, an Admiral of the Seas,
and deeply pensive Browne, attending
with remembered histories, to bring
a forgotten city back to life.

Hobgoblins, the bent-backed hippogryph,
shy Columbine, and wide-eyed Lazarus,
a leering Crocodile, the Hatter, Scaramouch,
the Whale, the Claw-toed Wolf-Boy;
all asleep, in character, ready to be called;
each, another haunting from Delphi
by way of Ephesus, or Callanais or Coventry:
The one perpetual fire, that never fails to prove,
imagination is the heart at play.

Players
A Birthday Poem For Robert Petty

Alone and silent, in a pool of light,
    with gentle frown and walrus eyes
    he works at the long pause, plays
    on our half-remembered past,
                conjures a feeling of community.

This strange capacity of players, to lift pain
    to render us, more or less becoming,
        this other kind of alchemy, deserves acclaim.

Let's sing for them, from Arden to the corners
    of the globe, who put aside printed words,
    commit hard lines to memory; delivering,
    out of paint and dust and fear, the passion of a play,
        the heart's atonement, all in all.

The Zen Of Sail ~ *for Tim*

Begins

with the serenity of letting go;

the simultaneous feel of movement in stillness.

Observe the conversations of water, how they change.

Wind on your face, grey riffle on the wave; a single voice.

You are the seed within the larch, at one with the breeze.

Breathe in the dry sweetness of oiled wood. Assess and decide

how to achieve a balance between surge and lift.

To make use of the inevitable is to be ready

for a safe anchorage,

a homecoming.

Argyll Farewell
for Bill & Barbara Summers

Are the lamps trimmed
at Tigh Ghaidheil ?

And does the west wind,
as it heaves over Inntreadh,
finger the sill, and send
the wood smoke downhill
to Ceanna Mor ?

And does the iron stove
draw well upon the logs
you cut and hauled together,
from the wood of Coinnich ?

May the dark season
be kind to you both,
and brief. May we meet again
to share a story and a dram,
in summertime, at Tigh Ghaidheil.

Author's Notes

CAVALIRI DI SAN MARCO These four bronze horses form the only Quadriga of classical antiquity still in existence. In the early middle ages they stood on the towers of the hippodrome in Constantinople. After the sack of the city by crusaders, they were shipped in 1203 to Venice. With the fall of the Republic in 1797, Napoleon ordered them to Paris to adorn the *Arc du Carrousel*. They were brought back to Venice in 1815.

DROPPING THE PILOT Russell Bower, Poet, Author, Educationist, Boatman and friend, was for many years, convener of The Bungay Poets' Group. This poem was written to mark his retirement from the post.

POCAHONTAS IN LUDGATE In Bradford in 1987, members of the Fairfax Community School History Workshop revealed to me the close links between the school site and nearby Bolling Hall, sometime home of the Rolfe dynasty. This led to correspondence with historians and 'descendants' in America, to David Garnett's fine novel, to Ben Jonson, ramblings around London and Gravesend, and finally to the Bradford City Library, for research, contemplation and writing.
The Epigraphs:
I & III – "Peace" speaks in the Masque, "Visions of Delight" – Ben Jonson. Performed at Whitehall, on or just after Twelfth Night 1617.
IV – from "A Staple of News" – Ben Jonson 1626/7.
V – "Wonder" speaks in "Visions of Delight".
VI & VII – Pocahontas, as set down.

HOW TO COOK A WHALE 'found poem'. Lucy Ho Miska-nis was of the Kwakwaka'wakw people, a group of 30 related tribes living along the rugged shores of Queen Charlotte Sound, on the N.E. coast of Vancouver Island. She was married to George Hunt, who at the turn of the century, researched and collected volumes of information on the lore and mythology of the Kwakwaka'wakw Peoples. With acknowledgements to Pat Kramer, who adapted the original for *Beautiful British Columbia* Magazine, Spring edition of 1999, whose account I plundered.

INSIDE THE HOLLOW HILL I have visited coal mines in Co. Durham, Staffordshire and Shropshire. The poem derives from these mortifying experiences and from long conversations with Jack Smart, Pit Deputy at Madeley Colliery in Shropshire.

THE SEA IS COMING BACK A poem with roots in Iman Wilkens' *Where Troy Once Stood* & numerous wanderings in The Gog Magog Hills, and the The Fen Country.

IRON BRIDGE The Army of the Great Reserve is Fredrick Engels' term for the mass of unemployed landless itinerant workers, as much a feature of a 'flexible economy' as it was of the industrial economy.

YARN HILL The term "Cenamagni". The root of this expression can be found in Julius Caesar's "De Bello Gallico" where he uses the term "Ceni Magni" for the whole territory of the Iceni (most of Norfolk and some parts of Suffolk). At what point Caesar's words were conflated/bastardised is unclear. The resulting "Cenamagni" having a swing of its own, seems now to appeal only to poets and songwriters.

DJINN (Baghdad 2.30am March 19th 2003) The moment of impact, first coalition missile, Gulf War II.

THE PEARL OF ORINSAY Poem to celebrate the Pearl Wedding of Nellie and Kenny Kennedy of Orasaigh, Isle of Lewis August xxiii 2002.
Long Life to Them Both!

Mike Bannister   June 2007